Do Lizards Have Lips?
And Other Tall Tales
from Toronto, Kansas!

Iris Craver

Ice Cube Press, LLC
North Liberty, Iowa, USA

Do Lizards Have Lips?
And Other Tall Tales from Toronto, Kansas!

Copyright © 2023 Iris Craver

ISBN 9781948509428

Library of Congress Control Number: 2022952087

Ice Cube Press, LLC (Est. 1991)
1180 Hauer Drive, North Liberty, Iowa 52317 USA
www.icecubepress.com steve@icecubepress.com
Check us out on Facebook and Twitter

The paper used in this publication meets the minimum requirements of the American National Standard for Information Sciences—Permanence of Paper for Printed Library Materials, ANSI Z39.48-1992.

Made with recycled paper.

Manufactured in USA.

"Kansas" by Naomi Shihab Nye reprinted by permission of the author, Naomi Shihab Nye, 2022. From *Words Under the Words*, Far Corner Books, 1995.

Dedication

This book is dedicated to the residents of Toronto, Kansas. I spent many years hiding out there and the place became dear to my heart. I am also dedicating these stories to my good friend, Dianna Palos, who introduced me to the pleasures of Cross Timber State Park and, of course, Lizard Lips! And finally, I am dedicating all of these tall tales to Dianna's good friend, Jean Marie Dancer. You will learn more about her later in the book. She just recently passed away on December 11, 2021. I would have worked harder to finish this collection before she left us if I had known.

3-29-23
Di — I hold you personally responsible for this book. Who knew...?!? Thank you for all the good times! Love you, Iris

Acknowledgments

Special thanks to my sister, Carole Connet for editing and my husband, Steve Stemmerman for design advice. Both held my hand and encouraged me all along the way. I would also like to especially thank the members of The Second Sunday Go Forth Writing Group. We have been meeting for years and usually, I would write poetry, but a while back my Muse teased out these tall tales about Lizard Lips. The group laughed and continued to laugh so I sort of hold them responsible. Our group leader, Katherine Greene, helped me figure out how to do the pencil sketch illustrations.

Jean Marie Dancer

Lizard Lips succeeds, $5 at a time

■ The Kansas Sampler Foundation has urged 1,000 of its members to go spend $5 apiece at the rural deli to give it a needed boost.

BY STAN FINGER
The Wichita Eagle

Bursting through the door with a carful of friends, one woman blurted, "We're here to save you!"

Another woman talked her tour bus driver into stopping when she realized they'd be passing by, and the passengers packed the place.

And then there was the grandmother from Kansas City who gave her granddaughter five bucks and marching orders: spend it at Lizard Lips Grill and Deli, just outside Toronto, Kan. on U.S. 54 about 90 miles east of Wichita.

"It's been remarkable," said Linda Geffert, co-owner of the eatery with attitude. "It's taken on a life of its own."

Lizard Lips was the first business selected for the Kansas Sampler Foundation's project to save struggling small-town enterprises by urging 1,000 of its members to spend $5 apiece at the store.

Lizard Lips is a combination gas station, convenience store and cafe, offering T-shirts, candy and humor as it dishes out home-cooked food. It offers a simple, unpretentious ambiance not unlike slipping into a favorite flannel shirt or a well-broken-in pair of shoes.

Halfway through the inaugural one-year effort, nearly 600 members have sent the pledge — along with scores of other people who are not members but heard about the effort through the media or friends.

"I'm really thrilled with the snowball effect," said Marci Penner, president of the foundation, which promotes and preserves rural culture. "I'm also really intrigued with how good people are feeling about helping. They go spend their five bucks, and they let me know they feel really good about it."

Lizard Lips sits atop a hill overlooking the Flint Hills. That isolation adds to its appeal — and subtracts from its bottom line.

Without enough volume to purchase prod-

ucts at cheaper bulk prices, the store struggles to get by each year. And with increasing minimum purchases needed to access suppliers, that challenge continues to get tougher for small stores such as Geffert's.

Geffert said the foundation's project has been just the kind of kick-start her business needed — and not just from the infusion of cash.

"The awareness in our local trade area has definitely increased," she said. "Some have

rediscovered us, and others have found us for the first time.

"We are actually building on a sustainable base here — people within a 50-mile radius of us," Geffert said. "Those are the ones who will come back once a month, twice a month."

It's the new faces that prove interesting, however.

Geffert said one woman who moved to southeast Kansas told her about family and friends back home in Philadelphia who can't

believe she could be happy where she is. Her answer is to cite places like Lizard Lips.

"There's just nothing like this left in Philadelphia and in that whole area," Geffert said, quoting the woman. "You can't find places like that in the big cities."

Ellen Morgan, who drove to Lizard Lips from Salina one Saturday afternoon, found the cafe irresistibly inviting.

Please see LIZARD LIPS, Page 22A

Lillian Hall cuts a sandwich at Lizard Lips Grill and Deli in Toronto, Kan. The cafe's ambiance and home-cooked food is a favorite of a small group of regulars, but the isolation that helps create its charm has also been a millstone for profits. The Kansas Sampler Foundation has urged its 1,000 members to go spend $5 each at the store to give it a needed boost. The response halfway through the project has exceeded expectations.

Mike Hutmacher/The Wichita Eagle

"You just feel at home. It was amazing to sit there and watch all the people come in — such a mix of people. Some of them were in suits, some of them looked like they were just up from the lake."

Ellen Morgan, who drove to Lizard Lips from Salina one Saturday afternoon

LIZARD LIPS
From Page 17A

"You just feel at home," Morgan said. "It was amazing to sit there and watch all the people come in — such a mix of people. Some of them looked like they were just up from the lake."

The store — and the effort to help preserve it — has struck a chord with the public. People are sending money even if they can't make it to Toronto, Geffert said.

One woman sent a check and a note about how, when she was a child decades ago, it was exciting to pass through a town and find a store with the same name as one back home.

Now, in this era of franchising, it's exciting to find a store that's different.

"The uniqueness is slipping away from us," she said. "Just to rediscover the uniqueness of places like this is important."

The project is working so well that Penner and the Kansas Sampler Foundation will expand the effort in 2001 to eight different businesses — one for each of the elements of rural culture identified by the foundation: architecture, art, commerce, cuisine, customs, geography, history and people.

"It's always fun to talk to Linda

because she's always got a new story that's unfolding to her," Penner said. "You can take all the fluff away, and what it comes

down to is you can give three owners hope that they can keep their small store alive, which is their dream. And all they had to do is

spend five bucks."

Reach Stan Finger at 268-6437 or sfinger@wichitaeagle.com.

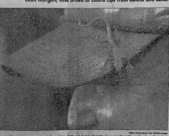
Lyman Hershberger, a regular at Lizard Lips Grill and Deli in Toronto, Kan., sports a clip-on lizard on the bill of his cap. "I couldn't live without this place," he said.

Mike Hutmacher/The Wichita Eagle

Waitress Shirley Fishel serves a crew of telephone linemen who are regulars at Lizard Lips Grill and Deli in Toronto. The down-home cafe was the first business selected by the Kansas Sampler Foundation for a project to give ailing small-town enterprises a boost by having its members visit and spend money.

Mike Hutmacher/The Wichita Eagle

CATCH UP! With recipes, entertaining and food ideas in Wednesday's Food section. The Wichita Eagle

Welcome to Lizard Lips!

Outside Toronto, Kansas, just down the road from Yates Center on U.S. Route 54 and halfway to Eureka, Lizard Lips is the local gathering place to get a hot lunch. Fried chicken with mashed potatoes, green beans, a dinner roll, and pie on Sundays. You can catch up on gossip or pick up some bait. Small jigs for the huge bottom feeder carp. Folks round here cut off the heads and stick 'em on fence posts. Get yourself some sandwich fixins. With some Budweiser, Wonder Bread, Miracle Whip, and Ham Salad to throw in the cooler. Then, head on over to Toronto Lake for the day. The owner, Carlene, has been trying to sell the place for at least 15 years. No luck yet. I asked her why she named the joint, Lizard Lips. She grinned. When she and her cousin bought the place, it was crawling with lizards! They were scrubbing and sweeping and fancying the place up when her cousin asked, "Do Lizards have Lips?" It stuck and forever more the place is known far and wide as Lizard Lips. Anyway, to get to Toronto Lake from Lizard Lips, you gotta go through the town of Toronto (population 281). Toronto still has a bank,

a post office, a liquor store, a senior center, and if you can believe it, a lumber yard. Homer's grocery store closed, crushed by the Great Recession of 2008. Nowadays, you'll likely see a few pickup trucks, with wet dogs hanging out the back, driving real slow down Main Street, coming home from a day at the lake.

To get to Toronto, the town, from Lizard Lips, turn south on State Highway 105, crossing over the Verdigris River, past the grove of pecan trees and the Cowboy Church. The Cowboy Church has an arena for rodeo events and baptisms are done in a stock tank. There's no passing of the collection plate, just throw your dollars in the boot by the door. Sermons are short and simple. Verna Thompson gives away little crocheted angels to visitors. You can get Verna's angels at the Toronto Senior Center too.

The Cowboy Church don't hold a candle next to the Methodist Church on State Street, one block from downtown Toronto, however, when it comes to pie, those Methodist ladies still serve the best pie by the slice anywhere around. Hwy 105 runs smack into the town of Toronto. Sissy's restaurant is the hot spot in town. She bought the building for $500 and lives upstairs. It is by reservation only and people come all the way from Emporia and Wichita for dinner. It's quaint. The library is directly across the street, next to the liquor store. You can get DVD movies at the library, pick up a 6 pack, and have a Saturday night. That's about it for Toronto. Oh, and a car wash. I almost forgot. There's a charming antique store too. When

11

you're heading back east and at the edge of town, take that right at the intersection where the little house sits and you can get a homemade dream catcher for $25.

Dianna

Now you are at the lake. Surrounded by Black Jack oaks. Dianna cherished campsite #50 where she languished at sunset. Wait a minute! Dianna is one of the main characters in these stories. I didn't mean to abruptly insert her here. It's just that I can't really separate Toronto Lake from Di. She's the one who gave me years of pleasure in this out-of-the-way place. Her Daddy had a fishing shack down near Tahlequah, Oklahoma, when she was growing up. He worked hard as a plumber and he played hard at his fishing shack too. When Dianna got her children grown up enough, she got herself a fishing shack, a juke joint, an artist studio, and a play house all for only $3,000 in Toronto, Kansas. Just one mile down the road from the lake.

It's about an hour and a half drive from my home down to Di's shack in Toronto. And it's about a full-blown head trip there and back. Spending 24 hours there scrapes the crap from your mind. There's really not much to do. Cooking is good. Throwing the I Ching can pass the time for an afternoon. Oh, and you can drive to Eureka to the Alco store to pick up rag rugs for 5 bucks. Another idea is to bring your old family picture albums from home and try to remember stories. Telling stories is a favorite pastime in my family. Some are true and others, well, others are just flat-out lies. One day, sitting on a blanket in the backyard at Di's hideout, I thought all the pictures in the album were upside down 'till I realized I was holding it upside down. This is the way of things when spending time in Toronto, Kansas. Things seem upside down or inside out or backwater backward. It reminds me of that song the grandkids love, "If the world were upside down, things would be different." Well, things ARE different in Toronto. When you come home from down at the Toronto beach (we call it a beach, but it's more like a muddy bank with some sand dumped every year by the Kansas Parks Department, sand likely dredged out of the Neosho River down the road) when you come home, you got to turn everything inside out to get rid of the sand, otherwise, the whole shack would've, over time, turned into a sandpile of sorts. When you first arrive, if nobody's been there for a month or so, you must turn everything inside out and upside down to shake out the brown recluse spiders. If you do get bit, take some of that plantain growing in the driveway out back, chew up a leaf, and slap a poultice on the bite for quick relief.

14

Dianna. You can't get that woman out of the kitchen. No matter where she goes, she throws a dish rag over her shoulder, grabs a chef's knife, and starts in chopping and prepping - onions, garlic, tomatoes, and cilantro for salsa. Toronto is no exception. The cabinet is well stocked with cumin, coriander, basil, thyme, parsley, rosemary, sage, marjoram, pepper, Himalayan salt, and all manner of vinegar, sauces, and spices to please the most discerning gourmand. It was a great delight for my brother, Big John, to spend time with Dianna, comparing recipes. He weighed in at 400 pounds and laughed, belly laughed, about being a foodie. He never made it down to Toronto before his death. His wife was jealous and wouldn't put up with him paying a visit to Dianna, especially off in some out-of-the-way place like Toronto. Too romantic. Little did she know.

A Weekend Getaway

Taking a nap down in Toronto was one of the main reasons to go for a weekend getaway. You pack up Friday, late afternoon, and depending on the season, get there before dark. It depends too on how much time you spend, stopped, at Beto Junction, a large truck stop at the intersection of I-35 and Hwy 75. (Now, if I was from out east, instead of a lifelong Midwesterner, I'd say THE 35 or THE 75, rather than the way we do, at least here in Kansas). Beto Junction has GIGANTIC cinnamon rolls. Perfect start for a weekend in Toronto with lots of sugar and carbs. Naptime food, with butter. Packing for Toronto involves lots of bags, in order of importance:

1. Bookbag, including journal
2. Snack bag, mostly chocolate
3. Swim bag
4. Food bag. Eggs, bacon, and potatoes for breakfast. Again, good napping food which means lots of good bakery bread. Lots of cheese such as brie, camembert, gjetost, and gruyere. You know. All the really good cheeses. Grapes and blueberries and pickles. Pasta and

pie for dinner. We preferred to bring our own pies to Toronto. As mentioned previously, the Methodist Church ladies make pie to die for.

However, the story about that one time when Happy Go Lucky actually died after eating a piece of blueberry pie at the annual 4th of July Woodson County fair left us with a bad taste in our mouths! Oh, Happy's real name was Pappy Luck, but everyone always knew him as Happy Go Lucky. Well, until he died.

5. A Wu Wu bag to include tarot cards, the I Ching, Eckhardt Tolle books, incense, crystals, smudge, a pendulum, and Runes. As defined by the *Urban Dictionary*, "Wu Wu is excessively new-agey, interest in such things as astrology.

Non-scientific. Mystically inclined. Sometimes abbreviated simply as 'Wu.'" For example, "Oh my God, Tarot cards are totally Wu Wu!"

6. Game bag to include Scrabble, several decks of cards, and dominoes.

7. Supply bag. Basics like toilet paper, matches, sunscreen, bug repellent, snow scraper, and umbrella(season dependent)

8. A change of clothing – maybe.

THE MAGICIAN.

THE FOOL.

Old-Growth Forest

The trees around Toronto Lake are a surprise. Black Jack Oaks. The botanical name is *Quercus marilandica*. This is a small red oak common to the areas known as the Cross Timbers or Ecoregion 29, which runs through this little strip in southeast Kansas on through Oklahoma to Central Texas. The Cross Timbers delineate between the eastern forests and the Great Plains where trees, mostly Cottonwoods, and Juniper, are rarely found except along little ravines. These Black Jack Oaks are an old-growth forest. Too small and gnarled to harvest as lumber, these Oaks found in the Cross Timber woods around Toronto State Lake can be 200-400 years old. Washington Irving, in his book titled *A Tour of Prairies* written in 1835 notes that they "struggled through a forest of cast iron." During hunting season, it's best to stay away from the woods as you are likely to get shot, mistaken for a deer.

21

Déjà vu

It's almost too good to be true. Well, maybe good isn't the word. More like, it's almost too strange to be true. 'Course this whole book of tall tales is too strange to be true, I'm thinking. It's like that when I hit that first stop sign at the end of Hwy 105 coming into Toronto. I have always felt being there was like some sort of Déjà vu. Like I've lived here in a previous lifetime or other. I don't actually hit the stop sign with my car or my fist. I just stop. It's the only stop sign in town. I take some time stopped there, for a while, to relish the sense of this. Being in a town with only one stop sign. There are other towns with only one stop sign. Like Paris, France, for example. Is there a country western song about a one-stop-sign-town? If there ain't there outta be. I thought about calling this book *A One-Stop-Sign-Town*, but I like *Do Lizards Have Lips and Other Tall Tales from Toronto, Kansas* better.

The Jungle

Steve spent his childhood growing up in Toronto. He spent time making paths through the jungle of lambsquarters growing in the empty lot where the Hobbs Mansion once stood. J.H. Hobbs and his wife, Mary, were early to settle in Toronto, having fled Canada after the war. They were the ones who named the town. I can't think of how many times after telling someone I went to Toronto for the weekend, they assumed I must do business in Canada to make such a short trip. The only remnant of the Hobbs Mansion was the two concrete hitching posts; one marked Mary and the other J. H. Steve and his friends played jungle in the empty lot. Lions and tigers and bears hid behind the walnut tree. Having seen *The Wizard of Oz* yearly on TV like every other kid growing up in Kansas, the boys figured the lions and tigers and bears lived on walnuts and they marveled at the green hulls, chewed up and spit out over by the ditch lilies along the road. The boys spent lots of time fishing off the bridge over the Verdigris River at the end of Main Street. That bridge is now decrepit, and the road closed with a big sign – BRIDGE OUT. The seven-year-old boys smoked cigarettes stolen from their fathers. Most of them quit smoking by the time they turned 12, moving on to other vices by then like drinking beer.

Jean Marie Dancer

The last time I visited Toronto, I stood outside the empty building on Main Street that used to house their public library. Empty. I thought, well, at least there's still the Post Office and Senior Center. The pizza joint closed too. The Lakeside Flea Market was still open, so, of course, I made my way in through the cabinets and tables loaded with every sort of antique and vintage memorabilia anyone could pick up at a local farm auction. Family farms were disappearing just like the drive-in movie theaters and the soft-serve ice cream shops you could find on the edge of just about every town in Kansas. Barbara keeps the Flea Market open only because she and her husband, Gary, bought the building for $1,000. She don't need to pay rent. Utilities aren't much. Taxes run about $80 per year. She told me even though she makes almost enough to pay her bills and carry enough cash to the farm auctions to buy more quilts and plates and singing fish mailboxes for the shop, she might be closing up too. Most of the traffic heading to the lake over the summer don't stop. They do stop at the new Taylor's Bait and Tackle shop on the corner of Main and Washington where the car repair shop used to be. I wondered if Taylors Bait and Tackle would put Lizard Lips out of business, but Jean Marie assured me there was enough business to go around. Jean Marie was the first woman, other than my daughter, who'd ever kissed me on the lips. Maybe it's because she lived in California for 25 years. She grew up in Pittsburg, Kansas, and ran off to become a hippie out west, joining the exodus of youth from all over America during the 1960s. She hitchhiked. Hitchhikers were everywhere and you could get a ride if you hit it right, maybe all the way to Berkeley. Jean Marie returned to Toronto, tired of the California lifestyle.

She bought a house for a pittance and lived quite comfortably on the money she saved after years of working as a tour guide. She still took off once or twice a year to lead tours and then could enjoy her simple life in Toronto. She volunteered at the Senior Center and was active in the Toronto Boosters Club. She hosted bicyclists who were traveling across the country following the TransAmerica Bicycle Trail sponsored by the Adventure Cycling Association. The trail touches both the Atlantic Ocean in Virginia and the Pacific in Oregon. It winds through nine states and is about 4,218 miles. The trail takes you directly by Lizard Lips on the Highway outside of Toronto and

with just a short detour, cyclists enjoyed a welcome at Jean Marie's home complete with hot showers, a warm meal, good conversation, and the beginning of a lifelong friendship.

Jean Marie put Toronto, Kansas, on the map for hundreds of cyclists who shared her story with others along the trail. Jean Marie, a TransAmerica Bicycle Trail unofficial "Angel." She recalled the story about how one cyclist after 4,000 miles finally reached the East coast and then took a train back to Kansas City. The adventuring cyclist called his mother to say that he had reached the train station in Kansas City and would be riding his bike the 40 miles back home to

Lawrence, Kansas. The mother responded, "Oh dear! Do you want me to come pick you up? That's a long way to ride your bike!" "Uh, no, Mom, I just rode 4,000 miles! 40 miles is a walk in the park!"

The Blues Man

The singer marveled at the crowd. Having come from years of playing in smoke-filled dives just about everywhere, and in every bar, playing 12-bar blues all over Detroit. This crowd gathered in the garage next to Taylor's Bait Shop on the corner of Main and Washington streets in Toronto was nothing he had ever seen before. Folks that rarely came to town had turned out for the big 150th-anniversary celebration on the 4th of July for Toronto Days. There were men in overalls with farmer's tans and women in tight cut-off jeans, so short that their cheeks peaked out as they swayed to the band playing Lynyrd Skynyrd's "Free Bird." The blues man from Detroit played his heart out. His heart had grown weary from events that led to him taking this gig out here in the middle of nowhere. After playing a set of Robert Johnson, John Lee Hooker, and Muddy Waters, he whispered to the bass guitar man, "This don't look like Detroit, man!" They switched it up to Bruce Springstein, Waylon Jennings, and ZZ Top. The crowd went wild.

We Had Dreams

I wrote a letter to Mr. Glidewell asking if he would sell his house in Toronto to me. Dianna and I had dreams of turning the place into an artist's colony. We imagined all sorts of writers and sculptors and musicians and potters and painters and quilters buying up the town and communing together there along the Verdigris River, where the stars at night shine big in big night skies. So little light pollution there. Little noise pollution. Not much fertilizer pollution, being out in the Flint Hills, land not well suited for farming. It's pretty clean, other than the occasional meth lab explosion. We had dreams of filling the town with other dreamers. Plenty of space for everyone. The old school had great acoustics and each artist could have a whole classroom for a studio. We had dreams. The National Endowment for the Arts would grant us seed money and the Kansas Commission for the Humanities would bankroll the rest. This was before Governor Brownback. We called him Brownshirt. He acted like a Nazi trying to exterminate "those people," not with ovens, but a slower death with no access to health care due to his refusal to expand Medicaid. He also closed the State Commission for the Arts. When this happened, our dream of turning Toronto into an artist colony vanished just like the Stuckey restaurants that were ubiquitous in years gone by.

Five Finger Fillet

Gander and his wives were legendary in Woodson County. His real name was John Smith, but ever since he was a boy, everyone called him Gander and the nickname stuck. He never was sure why he was called Gander, but I suspect it was due to the fact that when he got a tickle in his nose or took to laughing hard, he honked like a goose. Gander was a regular at Bert's Tavern over in Yates Center and he was a pro at the popular bar game – Five Finger Fillet or what is sometimes called Stabber-Scotch. Place the palm of your hand down on the bar with the fingers splayed. Then, your bar mate attempts to stab back and forth between your fingers. Gander got a few scars to show for it. Otherwise, the only other unusual part of Gander's story was that he collected wives. At last count, he had had 27 wives. Not as many as Ziona, listed in *Ripley's Believe It or Not*, living in India with 39 wives, 94 children and 33 grandchildren. Gander was only 43 years old when he died, which averaged out to one wife each year since he was 16. He'd gone down to Oklahoma for the first time since the age of consent to marry there is only 16. No one was ever sure if he was married to more than one wife at a time. It became a badge of notoriety to marry Gander and women stood in line to claim the honor. And, yes, just as you might have suspected, he died in bed.

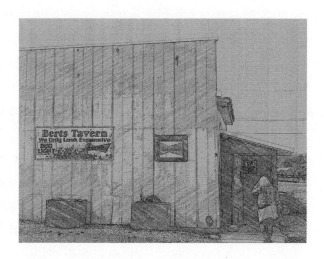

Snail Mail

The United States Post office still stands, freshly painted royal blue on Main Street next to the Senior Center. It is still open Monday-Friday from 8 AM-noon and Saturdays from 8-9:30 AM. Snail mail. People call it snail mail due to a common experience when it takes more than a week to get a social security or disability check. The snails in town, down by the river, have protested this derogatory language. They slither along the sidewalk joined by slugs, roly-poly bugs, and of course, lizards, holding signs reading, "Your life without snails will fail."

Desmond and Molly Jones

Seems like pretty much everyone in Kansas has packed up and headed west in the heat of the summer for a Colorado vacation. People in Toronto are no different except'n that some don't come back. Desmond and Molly ended up in Paonia, Colorado. It reminded them of home. They took one look and decided to buy up the old theater building and open a Beatlemania Museum. They had bands booked every weekend playing Beatles covers. Molly sings with all the bands. They sold John-Lennon-style glasses and little toy yellow submarines, octopi, and Rocky Racoons. Another Roadside Attraction listed the museum on it's website. Tourists came in droves. Desmond and Molly bought a little house down the street with a couple of kids in the yard. During the week, they opened a café in the front of the museum and called it "All My Lovin." People came to get married to the tune of "I Wanna Hold Your Hand" and "All You Need is Love." They printed postcards with the lyrics of "Imagine." Word got out. One day, arriving in a Cessna private plane, Paul McCartney and Ringo Starr stepped onto the tarmac at the Paonia airstrip. Their driver took them into the All My Lovin

Café and Beatlemania Museum. They autographed a few copies of *The White Album*, had a cup of tea, and left. To this day, no one believes it happened. If you ask Paul and Ringo, they simply replied, "If you want some fun, sing ob-la-di-ob-la-da!"

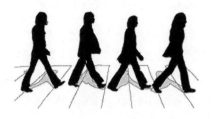

The Elder Dreamer Express

Going home after a weekend in Toronto is really hard.
Re-entry is tough. Just 24 hours away in what becomes
an altered state of consciousness, for me—it's hard to
wake up from the dream and head back to regular life.
After one last swim in the lake on a Sunday afternoon,
we would close up the place. Bundle up the trash. Make
sure the toilet wasn't running. Pack the perishables
from the fridge. Load up any rocks I'd scavenged on
a hike and hop aboard the Elder Dreamer Express.
The Elder Dreamer Express provides big sky scenery
through The Flint Hills of Kansas. The Express has no
set schedule. Really, all you gotta do is step into any
car or truck running back and forth between Lawrence
and Toronto, Kansas, breathe deeply and let your eyes
lose their focus. Like looking at those 3-D pictures
where suddenly an image pops out of the background,
but if you stop to think about it, it's gone. The Elder
Dreamer Express is like that. Surprises pop up out
of the Tall Grass Prairie. If you stop to think about
it, they're gone. One time, riding the Elder Dreamer
Express, I saw a triple rainbow, and no matter how far

39

down the road we went, there it was! A triple rainbow! Another time, I saw a moose. Surely it got lost and wandered away from Colorado to the Flint Hills.

Santa and Mrs. Claus

The Milky Way candy bars for sale at Lizard Lips gas station, bait shop, grocery, and deli are dusty. So are the cans of Chef Boyardee, Spam, deviled ham, and corn. Most of the time these items will sell before the expiration date, but if not, Carlene simply marks them ½ price and someone grabs them up.

Ever since Homer's Grocery closed some years back, to stock up, you've now got to head over to the closest grocery 20 miles away in Eureka, Kansas. One year, Santa and Mrs. Claus visited Eureka before the holidays. They walked along the street downtown, most buildings boarded up, and made their way to the Safeway store to pass out candy canes. Strangely enough, the people of Eureka seemed frightened of this jolly old elf and his missus. They covered their children's eyes and scurried off down the frozen food aisle, hoping to avoid any contact with St. Nick. Santa and Mrs. Claus laughed. Ho! Ho! Ho! In hopes of reassuring the Eurekans. To no avail. Mounting their sleigh, they flew off shouting one last time. "Merry Christmas to all and to all a good night!" The next day the plastic blow-up reindeer and Xmas trees collapsed all over town in Eureka and everyone in town found dusty cans of Chef Boyardee, Spam, deviled ham or corn in their stocking.

kris barlow

Tick. Tock. Tick. Tock. Tick. Tock. The electric clock in the old school building kept track of the time although no one ever set it for daylight savings. The building still had power since the gymnasium was regularly used for events like flea markets, potlucks, and fundraisers for whenever folks in town got a medical bill so high they'd lose what little they had. People pulled together and on a Saturday afternoon could raise $1,400 from selling $10 chances to win a quilt made by kris barlow, the local fabric fairy godmother. The money would go to someone who needed gallbladder surgery or a CPAP machine. kris barlow created quilts out of just about anything. When men could no longer button their shirts over their beer bellies, they'd bundle up a bag and leave them on kris' porch. Next thing you know, she'd whip up a quilt with appliques of each of the churches in town and hand 'em over to be auctioned, along with pies like when the Methodist church needed a new water line. One time, she made a quilt out of thin air. No one knew how she did it. These thin-air quilts were lightweight and nice for summertime picnics. You could see right through 'em.

The cyclists riding cross country loved those thin-air quilts for their backpacks. kris never charged a dime for those quilts. After all, being made from thin air!

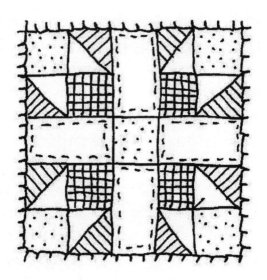

FOX News

Twila Fairfield was the woman who forgot herself. No one could remember when she arrived in Toronto and took up residence in the abandoned house over on Grand Street. She couldn't remember either. She didn't know how old she was or whether she ever had children. She didn't know her parents' names and she didn't have a Social Security card or a driver's license. She did have a bicycle and just like everyone else, she never forgot how to ride it and so she did. She rode that bike every day all over town, up to Stockton Street, over to Broad Street and back home. Sometimes, she'd forget where she was, but anyone who noticed her heading out toward Woodson County State Lake would stop, pick her up, throw the bike in the back of the truck and take her home. Twila couldn't remember if she ever went to school. She couldn't read or do arithmetic. She did have a TV and watched FOX news all day long (except when she was riding her bike). Some worried the FOX news stories would fill her head with foolishness, but it never was a concern 'cause Twila wouldn't remember any of it. She spent time feeding the birds and making pop-top jewelry.

45

Skinny Kenny

The nearest hospital is down the road in Eureka. It's a cold place. People round here rarely go. There are exceptions. Like when little Kenny shot his best friend, Harry, in the leg when they were nine years old. He didn't much like it when his friend, who he called Hairy Harry, started calling him Skinny Kenny. So, he went out back where his daddy had his hide-out drinking shack and where his daddy kept all his guns, hunting knives, crossbows, slingshots, fishing tackle, and tools. He went out back and grabbed a rifle and shot his friend in the leg. Kenny's mama grabbed Hairy Harry and ran him over to the hospital in Eureka. He purty near bled to death, but after a time, Hairy Harry's leg healed up just fine and he even ended up playing quarterback in high school. Skinny Kenny was just a kid and back then, nobody paid it no mind that he'd shot his best friend on purpose. Hairy Harry and Skinny Kenny stayed best friends lifelong. After high school, Harry joined the Highway Patrol and Kenny became a stuntman out in L.A. He jumped out of helicopters and ran through burning buildings. Everyone in Toronto was full of pride over the success of that hometown boy. Down at Lizard Lips, they put up a photo of him and kept videos for rent of the movie where he had a bit part – "Sawdust Murders." Everyone remembered when he shot his best friend in the leg on purpose and now, he's a movie star!

Build a Wall!

The animals in Woodson County get together every few months when the seasons turn. They meet up by the little pond near Hwy 105 between Toronto State Lake and Coyville. It's some sort of strange parade if you happen upon this gathering in March, June, September, or December.

Turkey Vultures
Common 5-lined Skinks
Blue-winged Teals
Goatweed Leafwing
Blanchard's Cricket Frogs
American Coots
Woodhouse Toads
Yellow Garden Spiders
Easter Collard Lizards
Great Plains Rat Snakes
Muskrats
Woodchucks
Southern Bog Lemmings
Elliots Short-tailed Shrews
Great Blue Herons
Northern Cardinals

American Crows
Red-headed Woodpeckers
Barred Owls

Just like in *Winnie-the-Pooh*, Owl leads the meeting every few months when the seasons turn. The question to be addressed, this year, is about the Armadillos. An invasion of Armadillos. Convoys of Armadillos are coming up from the South. "Hoards!" screech the American Coots. "We best prepare to defend our territory!" hiss the Great Plains Rat Snakes. "Build a wall!" scream the Turkey Vultures. The crowd yells...
"What are these alien creatures?"
"These Armadillo lepers!"
"Armored Lepers"!
"All they do is sleep!"
"Build a moat"!
"Fill it with Alligators"!

Dance Lessons

Ida Webb taught just about every child in Toronto how to dance. She lived to be 103 and was still teaching dance up to the day she died. She taught four generations of Toto's (the nickname for the locals) ballet, tango, country and western two-step, and even modern experimental dance. (The Methodist women didn't care for the modern experimental dance, but they couldn't say a word given that Miss Webb had taught them tap dancing!) She lived across the street from the park and often, weather permitting, dance lessons would take place in that park which oddly never had a name. It's just The Park. Since Ida died last year, there was some talk about naming the park after her, but the local Republican County Commissioners won't have it due to the stories, whether they are true or not makes no difference, the stories are that late on Halloween night and around May Day Ida Webb used to dance naked in the park. Her house is now abandoned to the creeping woodbine vines, snakes, and mice. Everyone says it's haunted and you can hear Ida dancing to Dean Martin crooning "That's Amore" on a scratchy vinyl record playing in the parlor.

52

Kirby's Secret

After a few years, Dianna upgraded from The Shack in Toronto to The Mansion which she bought for all of $10K. The local up-to-no-good boys, four of them, got bored one summer day, drank some beers to muster up the courage, and broke into The Mansion, hearing the gossip of a gold and silver stash. They broke the door that was original from when the place was built in 1920. They broke the drawers to the built-in hutch. They threw books off the shelves and basically created all sorts of sorrowful hell. They didn't know about Kirby. Kirby took care of the place. Mowed the lawn, fixed holes in screen windows, and so on. Kirby didn't take no shit. He'd spent time in Nam. That day, when the boys were looking for treasure, tearing up the place, Kirby showed up with his John Deere riding lawnmower. Seeing the broken door, he lumbered up on the porch, standing 6'10" and weighing about 350 pounds. He looked in on the scene, went back out, and waited for them boys to show their faces. He chased them out of town on his John Deere riding lawnmower and they have never been seen since. It's Kirby's secret. Never told.

Victor and Martha

The distance between Chicago and Toronto, Kansas is 645 miles. It might as well be 645,000 miles. Even though both Chicago and Toronto are in the same country and people speak the same language, primarily English, that's pretty much all they share in common.

When Victor and Martha learned that Aunt Frances May Poffenbarger recently passed away, they loaded up their few possessions in backpacks and hitchhiked to Toronto. They got a lift from the Southside of Chicago to East St. Louis in a truck hauling bathroom fixtures. Then from East St. Louis, a nice elderly lady took them all the way to 31st and Troost in Kansas City, Missouri. She played Ella Fitzgerald CDs the whole time and it turned out she was Ella's niece. From Kansas City, they found a bus that shuttles migrant workers from Olathe to Wichita and paid $20 each. They got dumped off at Lizard Lips. Victor asked Carlene if they could get a taxi. Carlene explained that there were no taxis in Toronto. Victor asked about Uber. Nope, no Uber. What is the WiFi password for Lizard Lips? Nope, no WiFi. Victor and Martha shrugged their shoulders and walked back to the highway. They stuck out their

thumbs and caught a ride with two kids heading for Sante Fe, New Mexico, to work at Meow Wolf, "an arts production company that creates immersive, multimedia experiences that transport audiences of all ages into fantastic realms." Victor and Martha both got jobs there, working as janitors.

CHICAGO

Sweet Relief

The cottonwood trees growing along ravines in The Flint Hills north of Toronto have deep roots, some 20-30 feet deep roots, solid. The botanical name is *Populus deltoides*. It is the official Kansas state tree.

The pulp from the cottonwood is used to make the finest paper for stationery and beautifully hard-bound books. One of these fine publications was written in 1952 by Euphorbia Alma Johnson with the title *Sweet Relief*. The book, popular in its day, was a "how to" guide for ladies on getting relief from ailments such as:

Arthritis – Find an ant hill. Stick your arthritic joint in the ant hill until you are covered with bites. Your arthritis will no longer be painful.

Lice – Smother with either mayonnaise or coconut oil.

Warts – Cover the wart with duct tape for a week which will slowly suffocate the wart causing it to fall off.

Pinched nerves – Take 2-3 teaspoons of apple cider vinegar in warm water with a little honey. Drink twice a day.

Sore throats – Coat your throat with lard or chicken fat and then tie dirty socks around your throat overnight. You will feel better in the morning.

Headaches – Rub cow dung mixed with molasses on your temples.

Bites and infected wounds – Get a mad stone. Mad stones are found in the stomach of cud-chewing animals like cows or deer. Place the mad stone on the bite or wound and it will absorb the poison.

Menstrual cramps – Find a toad, burn it in a pot, and put the ashes in a small cloth bag. Strap the cloth bag between your legs. The ashes from the toad will relieve your cramps.

Age spots – Dab with buttermilk.

Corns and calluses – Crush five or six aspirins into a fine paste and mix with one-half teaspoon lemon juice and one-half teaspoon water. Dab the paste on your corns or calluses and cover with a piece of plastic wrap. Then cover the plastic with a heated towel. After 10 minutes, remove everything and gently scrub away the loosened skin with a pumice stone.

Whining children – Graham crackers and milk will soothe even the most difficult child.

Boredom – Make chocolate chip cookies.

Frigidity – Mix chopped-up garlic and onions in milk. Drink before bed as an aphrodisiac.

Melancholy – Take a sunbath every day while listening to classical music such as Bach, Beethoven, or Mozart.

Pneumonia – Make a mustard plaster by

mixing two Tablespoons of flour and one Tablespoon of dry mustard powder with one egg white. Take a washcloth folded in half and spread the mixture inside. Fold back in half again and safety pin to the outside of an old t-shirt in line with your chest. Wear it all night or all day long if home sickly. You will feel it pulling the congestion right out of your lungs.

Meddling mother-in-law – Give her a surprise vacation. The surprise is the one-way ticket.

Husbands who throw their dirty clothes on the floor next to the laundry hamper—move the dirty clothes to a pile on his side of the closet. When he runs out of something to wear and asks where his clothes are, tell him that you only wash dirty clothes that are in the hamper and explain that you thought the ones he threw on the floor weren't dirty so you put them back in the closet. On the floor!

Rumpledethumps

Joe Andy O'Callaghan is a big man, robust, clean-shaven. Except for a month before St. Patrick's Day when he grows out a beard, dyes it green, dons a green bowler hat, and green wool pants sent to him by his cousins over in the old country, the Emerald Isle, Ireland, County Kerry, where they live in the lovely town of Killarney. Joe Andy wears green suspenders over a t-shirt declaring "Erin Go Braugh," an expression of allegiance to Ireland, usually translated as "Ireland Forever." Now, Joe Andy has never set foot in Ireland, but don't let that make you no matter. Every year, he gets up before the crack of dawn on March 17th and paints the center line down Main Street in Toronto bright green. He sets up in front of the Senior Center with a boom box playing "Oh, Danny Boy" and "Too-Ra-Loo-Ra-Loo-Ra" all day while drinking green beer and handing out corn-beef with cabbage complete with Rumpledethumps* on a plate.

Last year, the Mayor of Killarney came to lead the annual St. Patty's Day parade and was awarded by Joe Andy a key to the city. Amidst all sorts of fanfare and good times to be had, Joe Andy and his precious twin grandchildren fell asleep on the bench in front of the bank. The next morning when Ernest Lee Frank (his actual legal given name) came to open the bank, finding Joe Andy and the kids asleep on the bench, he kindly called the sheriff who took them home before the Toronto Boosters Club turned out to clean up the trash left by all those who had enjoyed the festivities. Little Sean Brennan was surprised to find the key to the city left by the Mayor of Killarney on the steps of city hall. He had made a mad dash to meet his plane at Kansas City International Airport. Sean thought it his lucky day and hid the key to the city in a shoe box which he buried in his backyard.

*Recipe for Rumpledethumps
Ingredients:
1 pound boiled and mashed potatoes
1 pound boiled cabbage, drained
1-ounce butter (or margarine)
Salt and black pepper
Some folks (like Dianna) add carrots and turnips.
Method:
Mash the potatoes and finely chop the cabbage and mix in a large saucepan in which the butter has been melted. Keep the

saucepan over low heat to keep it hot. Season to taste and serve piping hot.

The mixture can also be put into a greased oven-proof dish and cooked at 400 degrees F/ until the top is browned.

Poison!

Out on the edge of town, the old lady, Diamond Watch (seriously, her given birth name) lived in a run-down little house surrounded by a garden full of poisonous plants. Protecting the back gate grew a large patch of Poke. Now, some confuse the purple poke berries with elderberries. Big Mistake! Poke (*Phytolacca americana*) is quite poisonous. Birds aren't bothered by it and spread the seeds widely in their poop. Some serious herbalists use dried poke berries to fight cancer. If it doesn't kill you, it might cure you. (Note. Please remember that this is a collection of Tall Tales and not meant to be medical advice of any fashion!) There's also a huge patch of Moonflowers (*Datura innoxia*), which spreads out over most of the backyard with big trumpet-like white flowers that open at night and spikey seed pods. Extremely toxic. Some shamans eat the seeds for ritual journeying. Toronto teenagers foolishly snuck in to eat the seeds as a psychedelic, but Sharon Armstrong and Karen Salsburg both ended up in the hospital, raving mad and never recovered, ending up living on the streets of Wichita, eating out of garbage cans.

Diamond tends a nice bunch of White Snake Root out front of her porch. Pretty white flowers. Its botanical name is *Ageratina altissima*. If a cow eats it, they're dead the next day. Abraham Lincoln's mother died from eating beef tainted with White Snake Root. Protecting the dog door on the side of the house, Black Nightshade stands with its five white petaled flowers in the perfect shape of a pentagon. Black Nightshade (*Solanum nigrum*) protects against wandering ghosts or induces them to visit depending on your needs. And, of course, very poisonous. Rue stands out by the shed. Its botanical name is *Ruta graveolens*. So delicate and pretty. Causes violent vomiting leading to death. Diamond enjoys her garden of protective poisonous plants. No one ever accused her of poisoning that man who shot her cat. He keeled over one day and his kids had him cremated just like that.

Giants

The stone beach at Toronto State Lake is mostly limestone and sandstone. Not sand. Sandstone. And clay. The bottom of the lake is mucky the first few steps out. And then it's nice and rocky. Smooth stones. Easy for Dianna to walk out into the lake, and plop on to her air mattress for what she called her "floaty-mat-therapy." She spent hours floating, listening to the voices from the stone outcroppings telling stories about the people who hid out in the Cross Timber Forest. The stones told the stories about the members of White Hair's band of the Osage Nation who frequently ventured to this area in the fall during hunting expeditions. Their village was south of what is now Toronto near Pumpkin Creek in the Verdigris Valley. The Osage people were giants. I mean, they stood easily 6-7 feet tall. They were so tall that they could easily reach up and grab a squirrel scampering along a tree branch. The Osage people were so tall that on a cloudy, rainy day, they could simply stand on their tippy toes and enjoy the sun. An Osage by the name of Pitatus, accidentally, one day, knocked her head into the moon creating a crater, she was so tall. They named the crater after her. Most people believe that James Naismith invented basketball, which contributed to the great success of the Jayhawks at the University of Kansas. Actually, basketball was invented by the Osage. One of the descendants of the Osage is now living in Altoona, Kansas, and operates the Prairie Nut Hut Bar and Grill which serves the tallest stack of pancakes, the tallest triple-patty hamburger, and the tallest 7-layer chocolate cake. They serve the tallest ice cream soda. Why, it's so tall, you have to climb up on a ladder to drink it.

The Pee Pee Sisters

Even when she was no longer able to take her own self to the bathroom, Bridget Brock wore pearls every day. She never did get the hang of wearing pantyhose and when girdles and garter belts fell out of fashion, she wore elastic banded hose under her skirts that modestly covered the scars on her legs from various surgeries trying to repair varicose veins and arthritic knees. Bridget loved taking day trips with her daughter. Once, in October, they set out on an adventure and ended up in Toronto. Bridget was slowly losing control of her bladder and well, by the time they got to town, well, Bridget really had to go. Her daughter stopped at Lizard Lips, got the wheelchair out of the car, loaded up her mother, and raced her in to find a toilet, barely negotiating the narrow hallway and lifting her mother out of the chair, pulling down her underpants, and landing her neatly on the commode. Bridget laughed the whole time and told the story about one time when she was younger out in the world with her lover. He made her laugh so much that she peed her pants. Come to find out that both of her sisters were prone to peeing their pants and they called themselves "The

Pee Pee Sisters." No joke. Every time Bridget told the story of The Pee Pee Sisters, she laughed so hard, she peed her pants.

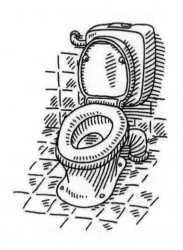

After You

Patrick walked to the lake every day from when he was five years old. Nobody gave him no mind. When he got old enough, rather than buying a car, he bought a motorboat. The girls loved to listen to Patrick tell jokes. One of his favorites went like this. "Did you hear about the band Kansas getting arrested for kidnapping at the airport? No, what happened? They tried to carry on my wayward son." Anyway, Patrick always told each girl, "I named my boat after you." The girl would giggle and ask if they could take a ride in the boat at sunset. Every girl was hoping for a romantic evening until they got out to the boat and saw the name of the boat painted proudly on the stern, "AFTER YOU." Sometimes it took a minute for the girl to get the joke.

Letters to Fred

To tell the truth, all of these stories about Toronto, Kansas, are just flat-out a bunch of lies. I don't know what possessed me to write up such lies other than the fact that I grew up in a family where telling lies was a valued skill. Anyone who could tell a good story was given lots of admiration. And, the more exaggeration, the better. Now, my Daddy, for example, spent years writing letters to his friend, Fred, who actually did not exist. Never mind. Daddy would write a letter to Fred and then he'd turn right around and write a letter to himself from Fred. I've got the whole collection stashed somewhere. I heard that a while back, Toronto had an election for the mayor. It turned out the Republicans didn't get anyone to run for the office, so the local die-hards entered the name of someone to be on the ballot who, I'm telling you, this person did not actually exist. Scotty Becket. Oh, the Republicans went to great lengths to support this fake candidate, scheduling rallies and chances for Beckett to meet with church congregations, the County Extension agents, The Toronto Boosters Club, and all manner of events designed to insure a landslide victory for Scotty. On

73

each occasion, it was announced that Scotty Beckett had to cancel at the last minute due to a bad attack of the stomach flu or a car broken down over by Cherrydale or the nursing home in Eureka called to say he better come quick to see his mother. On election day, sure enough, Scotty Beckett (R) won hands down. When it came time for him to assume office, the Republicans regretfully informed the community that he had drowned the night before in the lake and the sheriff was unable to retrieve the body. It just made sense then, that the sheriff, Jimmy Lyons (Not well-liked in these parts. He could never have run for mayor and won.) now serves as both sheriff and mayor. During his term of office, he accomplished nothing other than continuing to catch folks speeding out to the lake to go fishing and slapping them with big fat fines. He used money from the fines to install new carpeting in his "office." His "office" was also his home. All the Republicans hope he will serve a second term.

Every hour fishing
Adds an hour
to your life

CROSS TIMBERS

‹ TORONTO POINT
½M EAST   1½M SOUTH
CABINS   CAMPING   HIKING

‹ PARK OFFICE HOLIDAY HILL
9M EAST on 105

Cousin Flossie

Despite the best preparations, Jane was not ready for what happened the day her second cousin, Flossie, showed up for a visit. Flossie called from a pay phone near the Gates BBQ in Kansas City, telling Jane she would be there in about an hour. Just passing through on her way from East St. Louis to Oklahoma City. Some kinfolk there had invited her after learning that her home had burned to the ground. Jane hadn't seen her second cousin since they were children, being as her own parents were not prone to venturing far from Toronto. In fact, they had never been east of the Mississippi, or west of the Rockies. Well, Jane, being raised on the value of hospitality, set to work tidying up her home, one of the finest in Toronto, right next to the lumber yard. She vacuumed and real quick made a cobbler from the peaches she had in the freezer. Put on a pot of coffee and then heard the front doorbell and before having a chance to take off her apron, in barged Flossie smelling like cheap perfume, cigar smoke, and whiskey. Behind her was her traveling companion, Buck, hauling several very large hard-sided suitcases and a cooler. They tracked mud across the room and pulled up chairs at the kitchen table, each lighting up cigars and breaking out flasks to take a swig before slapping the table and swearing, "God Dammit, Jane! What the hell are you doing still living in this backwoods, nothing to do, crappy little town?!?!"

Six months later.

Flossie and Buck never left. To this day, you'll find them on Jane's front porch, smoking, drinking, and swearing.

The Glee Club

People, not from around these parts, were confused to find out that the Toronto Glee Club was NOT a small group of men sitting in the parlor singing acapella in four-part harmony. No, not even close. The Toronto Glee Club was named after one of the town's most civic-minded residents, Glee Fully. Her parents thought such a name would lead their precious girl to a life of fun and festivities and, sure enough, Glee Fully was planning social events from the time she was old enough to make a phone call. Why, she was the founder of Toronto Days for the 4th of July. She made sure the Easter Bunny delivered lots of eggs every year out at the Woodson County Fairgrounds. Glee was THE wedding planner for miles around. She dressed up as a clown for birthdays. Well, you get the picture. Then one day back in 1987, a trucker rolled into town by the name of Honest Lee. It was love at first sight and before you could clean your plate, Honest Lee escaped with Glee and they've never looked back. Their girl did come to town once to visit her aging grandmother. The child's name was Fortunate Lee.

WOODSON COUNTY
KANSAS

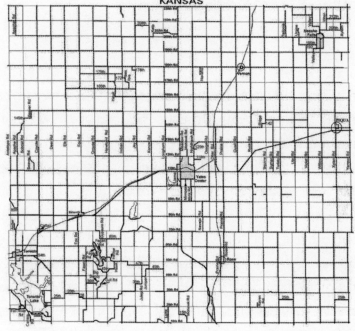

The Pain Drain

Dr. Chris comes to Toronto once a month and performs all manner of healing practices for anyone with an appointment and enough cash. Dr. Chris has real licenses from the Ithaca School of Herbal Medicine, The New Testament Institute for Healing Touch, the Cleveland Chiropractic College, the Breitenbach Hydrotherapy School, and more. He can determine if you are low on magnesium just from smelling your breath. Dianna knew pain. She carried pain. She was up close and personal with pain. Time spent in Toronto was pain medicine. On a fairly regular basis, Dianna would meet with Dr. Chris for a Pain Drain. He would stand behind her and visualize healing energy flowing through his body. He would scan her body to find any throbbing or tingling areas. This would typically be the back of her neck. Dr. Chris would then place his left hand on her neck and let his right hand hang down and away from her body. This would allow the pain to drain. Finally, he would switch hands, placing his right hand on her neck and holding his left hand in the air. This would bring healing energy from the Source to fill the void left by the Pain Drain. After several of these treatments, Dianna decided to stop. The problem was that now whenever she turned her neck, she got diarrhea.

The Sewing Club

Once a month, the ladies from the Sewing Club in Toronto would load up in Mitzi's van, all eight of them, and take a road trip to Beto Junction at the intersection of I-35 and 75 Hwy, about 40 miles north of Yates Center. Beto Junction is one of those gigantic truck stops complete with showers and all the necessary trucker supplies, including a ready stream of truck stop prostitutes who serviced their more basic needs. The Sewing Club liked to go for lunch, which meant chicken fried steak with mashed potatoes and gravy and corn. All the ladies liked the strong coffee, black, and cinnamon rolls the size of a dinner plate. Recently, the kitchen had added chili to the menu and Linda made that her regular. Chili with a side order of a dinner-plate-sized cinnamon roll. Now, Linda wasn't really as much into the fabric arts as the rest of the gals. She just liked the company. Sewing Club was more of a social event for her. She'd make an effort by bringing in her husband's shirts that needed buttons sewed back on. That was as far as she could go and Mitzi had to thread her needle for her. Linda could take up the whole afternoon complaining about her life. She'd start in on her husband as she sewed buttons on his shirt. Most women would give their right arm for a man like Linda's husband. He'd fix toilets, change the oil in the car, clean storm windows, build raised beds for the garden and re-roof the house. But according to Linda, he never did it fast enough or quite right. One day, when Linda's husband went to Wichita to get a better deal on tires for their Suburban, he met a woman working the counter at the Firestone shop. She'd lost her right arm in an accident after driving on worn-out tires and devoted herself to doing whatever she could to help people make sure their tires had adequate tread. Linda's husband and the one-armed tire sales lady hit it off and he never came back home. Last Linda heard, he and the one-armed lady were enjoying long road trips with good tires, going around the country to tire dealer conventions. Linda told The Sewing Club all about it over strong coffee at The Beto Junction truck stop.

Mrs. Piggle Wiggle

When Sara was growing up there was still a school in Toronto. When it closed, the children all had to take a bus 15 miles to the nearest school in Yates Center. She loved reading the books about Mrs. Piggle Wiggle. She especially loved the story about Mrs. Piggle Wiggle knitting mittens for children from a ball of yarn that tasted like vanilla. Or, she'd knit scarves you could eat that tasted like chocolate. Well, of course, Sara knew these were just stories, like a fairy tale or a tall tale, but she couldn't ever let go of the idea and the wonder of it. She spent hours in her kitchen trying out formulas of red and white striped peppermint-flavored yarn and brilliant lemon-flavored thread. She'd stay up into the wee hours of the morning stirring up batches of delicate cloth for making teddy bears that could be eaten tasting like brown sugar. One night, there was a terrible storm with hail and loud long rolls of thunder. Lightening hit Sara when she went out to hang her apple-flavored bandanas on the clothesline. Sara was thrown to the ground and lay there in the pounding rain till the next morning. When she awoke, she pulled out her hanky to blow her nose. Her hanky smelled like cotton candy.

She took a bite. Her hanky tasted like cotton candy. She ate her whole hanky. Excitedly, she drove over to Lizard Lips to tell her news to whoever might be there that Thursday enjoying a hot roast beef sandwich. Leonard, who worked for the Highway Department, mowing the grass for miles, was there picking up a pack of cigarettes, although he told his children he'd quit. When they smelled smoke on him, he'd lie and say he gave a ride to a hitchhiker who was smoking. Anyway, Sara, full of excitement, offered Leonard a red bandana. Try it! It tastes like strawberry! You can eat it or use it as a headband! Leonard's mouth dropped open. He left in a hurry and as soon as he got out to his tractor, lit up a smoke and drove off down the highway, shaking his head. Undeterred, Sara knitted a pair of mittens that tasted like marinara sauce and sent them to Senator Bernie Sanders.

Lizard Lips Grill & Deli
OPEN 7am to 6:30 pm

TODAY - Reuben + Chips + Pickle $6.00

THURS. - Hot Ham & Cheese Sandwich

FRIDAY - Fishwich + Fries

SAT. - Menu

SUNDAY - 9/19 PORK CHOPS +
    Cheeto Mac 'n' Cheese +
    Cacio e Pepe Brussells Sprouts +
    Fresh Veggie Medley + Garlic Bread +
    Pistachio Cream Pie
        with Coffee or Tea

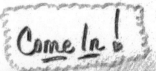
Come In!

The Boot

Now, Gerald, who owned Lizard Lips with his sister, Carlene, specialized in telling fishing stories. Being as he sold the only bait and tackle supplies in these parts for years. There was the one about Danny from over in Cherrydale who caught a boot at the lake. Turned out to be the boot of Francine Miller who'd gone missing ten years ago. Her boyfriend, Travis, roughed her up one night and not wanting her bruises to draw attention, tied her up and threw her in the lake. Travis forgot to tie her boots very well, and well, Danny caught her boot using just a worm on a hook. He brought the boot to Lizard Lips to show off and, sure enough, Francine was Gerald's cousin and he'd seen her wear those fancy leather boots at all the family get-togethers. The boyfriend showed up missing after the DNA test showed positive. Some say Gerald and Danny tied up Travis real good, making sure to put some cement in his boots and dumped him in the lake. He wasn't "the one that got away."

Seedy Sam

He was the local, Woodson County, version of Johnny Appleseed. Everyone in these parts knew him as Seedy Sam. He had a sordid past, trying to start a pornography business out of his garage at the edge of town. His porn business failed. He just couldn't keep up with the technology. Sam's only other interest, other than porn, was growing vegetables. Why, that man grew pumpkins as big as pig pens and corn that really did grow higher than an elephant's eye. Sam took to saving his seeds and had pockets full to give away. All this happened a long time ago, but Toto's still save their Seedy Sam seeds and enter tomatoes big as grapefruits in the county fair. When asked for his garden secrets, he'd swear it was Jesus helping him make up for his sinful ways. Planting seeds. No longer sowing his seed.

Winter Wind Blizzards

One year, Dianna didn't have a place to live, between divorce and new grandchildren, so she moved to Toronto sort of permanent like. It was a bad winter and the snow piled up to where she couldn't even open the doors to get out. Wouldn't have made much difference. Snow drifts, some a good 3-4 feet tall, piled up. The wind in Kansas is well known. Even people in Moscow, Russia, know of tornadoes and the Wizard of Oz. Not even Ford F-150s could negotiate the streets of Toronto that winter unless they had a snow plow. Some local men did get out and make a path down Main Street, but if you lived even a block away, you couldn't get there by car. After a few days, pent up, Dianna ventured out, ready to walk to Lizard Lips, about 3 miles away. This did not go well. The temperature hovered at 9 degrees Fahrenheit with a windchill of -20. Remember. Kansas. Wind. Tornadoes are devasting. Kansas Winter Wind Blizzards are devastating too. Tornadoes will suck the rings right off your fingers and throw them down on the sidewalk in front of the post office in the next county over. You can't even SEE the rings on your fingers in a Kansas

Winter Wind Blizzard. I've wondered why Dairy Queen called their sweet delights, Blizzards. Kansas Winter Wind Blizzards are not sweet or delightful. The closest Dairy Queen for Toronto is up the road in Emporia. The Tip Top in Yates Center beats Dairy Queen if you ask me. No Blizzards on their menu! Perhaps being locally owned, they know about Kansas Winter Wind Blizzards. Tip Top just has your traditional root beer floats and hot fudge sundaes. Dianna made it about 9 blocks in the Kansas Winter Wind Blizzard. She couldn't see a thing. All of a sudden, Big Foot (also known as Sasquatch) picked her up and took her back home. The Kansas Department of Wildlife and Parks has denied the possibility explaining that Toronto is just too far south for Big Foot who is noted to only be sighted in the Pacific Northwest. The park ranger for the Cross Timbers State Park, when contacted by the *Woodson County Journal*, said, "No comment".

Pirate Spiders

On the longest day of the year, the pirate spiders cast off down the Verdigris River to lay a raid in the wildflower patch growing near the cow shed owned by Homer's son, Tom. The pirate spiders heard tell about sunflowers there bursting with pollen and bee balm and coneflowers and chicory. These flowers had migrated out to Tom's cow shed for the dirt. Fertile. Years of manure. Bug heaven! Every sort of pollinator lingered around Tom's cow shed and other spiders too. In the dark of night, the pirate spiders spun webs under the cow shed eaves and between the sunflowers. They hung off the fences and all around the yard light kept on at night to scare off predators, keeping the chickens, who lived in the cow shed, safe. Now you likely are thinking that those pirate spiders feasted on flies and gnats. Oh no, pirate spiders eat OTHER SPIDERS! Cannibal spiders.

Toronto not only has cannibal spiders but stories of people who eat people. Igor Yuremeyev met a young Kansas woman who was on a professional exchange tour with journalists in Moscow. They flirted and ended up married. Igor and his wife settled in Toronto after she got a job as an adjunct instructor at Emporia State University. He busied himself successfully making pelmeni and selling it out of the deli at Lizard Lips. Pelmeni are dumplings often considered the national dish of Russia. Typically, they are stuffed with a filling of ground pork, chicken, turkey, or beef. Igor and Amy had a big fight one day. Likely a result of a breakdown in communication and an inability to negotiate some cultural differences. Igor killed Amy in a fit of rage, and ground her up to stuff pelmeni which he kept in the freezer and ate for several months before human bones were found out back of his shed and local law enforcement put two and two together.

The Lost Poet

Kansas

    by Naomi Shihab Nye

Driving across the centre of Kansas
at midnight, we're talking about
all our regrets, the ones we didn't marry,
who married each other, who aren't happy,
who should have married us.
Ah, it's a tough world, you say,
taking the wrong road.
Signposts appear and vanish, ghostly,
ALTERNATE 74.
I'm not aware it's the wrong road,
I don't live here,
this is the flattest night in the world
and I just arrived.
Grain elevators startle us,
dark monuments
rimmed by light.
Later you pull over
and put your head on the wheel.
I'm lost, you moan. I have no idea where we are.
I pat your arm.
It's alright, I say.
Surely there's a turn-off up here somewhere.

My voice amazes me,
coming out of the silence,
a lit spoon,
here,
swallow this.

~ from *Words Under the Words* (The Eighth
Mountain Press, 1995)

Some old-timers in Toronto well remember the night
when poet Naomi Shihab Nye wandered, lost, and
ended up at Lizard Lips. Everyone was surprised when
she published her poem and changed it from Highway
54 to Highway 74.

Franny

The big secret in Yates Center, down the road to the east of Toronto about 12 miles, was the $1 lunch to be had at Franny's. There warn't no sign telling you where to find Franny's. You just had to know and if you were in the right place at the right time and held your mouth just so, a local would direct you to a non-descript door in an old building on the town square. Once inside, you went up about 100 stairs, took a right, and down a long dark hall, and there you'd find:

Taco salad on Mondays

Meatloaf on Tuesdays

Mac n cheese on Wednesdays

Spaghetti on Thursdays

Fish Sticks on Fridays

All for $1 and you just put it in the cash register yourself. The tricky part was the long shelf of pies! Three dollars a slice. Rhubarb, Gooseberry, Lemon Meringue, Cherry, and sometimes Pecan from the local pecan groves. I've been there many times and never laid an eye on Franny. Some said she had long gray hair hanging past her waist and wore lots of turquoise jewelry. Some say she was missing a foot. Others swore she was missing an eye and wore a patch. The guy at the gas station on the corner of Hwy 75 and 54 grinned and told me she was 105 years old and that as a girl she cooked for Buster Keaton before he'd gone off to be a silent movie star. One day, she just never showed up and the sign on the door simply said – CLOSED.

Drought

Stan was born and raised in Toronto. One year, there was a terrible drought. Stan took matters into his own hands. He built a bonfire as tall as the grain elevator down the road in Yates Center. When Stan set that gigantic stack on fire, the smoke created pyrocumulus clouds causing it to rain so heavy it filled up Toronto Lake too, flooding the campsites, even Dianna's favorite one #50. Thinking quick, Stan enlisted everyone he could find in town to bring their garden hoses out to the lake. The people of Toronto sucked on hoses siphoning flood water from the lake out to the Verdigris River. Why, that water rushed right on down to the drought-stricken Oolagah Lake in Oklahoma. They even interviewed Stan on The Weather Channel.

Canadian Geese

One moonlit night, Don was driving along trying to find just the right light to capture a photo of a flock of white Canadian geese who were migrating north after winter. He headed down a back road to Woodson County State Lake. Upon pulling into the parking lot, he found not a flock of white Canadian geese, but rather a gathering of white-hooded men burning a large wooden cross and shouting about preserving the purity of our country. Don had grown up out in Hays and he'd been around some pretty conservative Republican sort of folk, but words failed him when he thought he might have to speak to these cowards hiding behind their masks. He quickly snapped some photos and tore out of there faster than Trump can tweet!

Trouble

The day arrived. It was 1972 and the circus was coming to town. To Toronto, of all places! The Big John Strong Circus was on a tour of the Midwest, traveling along state highways. The circus stopped about every 100 miles and after a successful stint in Wichita, they made time for a short exhibition in Toronto on the way up north to Topeka. The local kids jumped up and down watching circus clowns and acrobats ride into town on camels, elephants, ostriches, and a donkey. Tommy was only 14, but he was already known by every sheriff, highway patrolman, or any other officer of the law as Trouble. People round here didn't even call him by his given Christian name anymore. They just called him Trouble. Here comes Trouble! And sure enough, Trouble would saunter into Lizard Lips and walk out with a bottle of Coca-Cola, a pocket full of chewing tobacco and bubblegum, and a Zippo lighter. Some he'd paid for. The lighter? Well, he'd just pocket the lighter. Tommy spent more time out of school than in. He'd back-talk the teachers and stick his foot out on purpose to trip the coach. Oh, he was Trouble. And then too, he'd gotten Betty knocked up. He was only

14 and she was 21. She took the baby and moved to Chicago to live with her cousin. Tommy was Trouble. Even when he was a little boy, he took scissors and cut all the hair off his sister's dolls. She cried 'till she turned blue. The circus packed up after two days. Two days of thrills and excitement. Two days of flame throwers and dancing monkeys. Two days of barrel juggling baboons and girls who would sing the American anthem while walking on their hands. Two days of cotton candy and fry bread. Two days of chameleons you could buy as a pet and they'd turn different colors. When the circus packed up after two days, Tommy Trouble packed up too. He never returned to Toronto and his parents said, "Good riddance." Word had it that he spent the rest of his short life traveling with that circus and died at the age of 34 when a human pyramid collapsed. Tommy was the frontman man on the pyramid. He faltered. The pyramid fell, killing Tommy and another man. Tommy was Trouble.

The Shiney J

Dianna's hideout out behind The Mansion is known as the Shiney J. After airing out the place, the Shiney J pulls you in and anything worrying you blows out toward the lake on the breeze. The place got its name from the Shiney family and the Jackson family. Mr. Shiney came along by marriage and he claimed the garage as storage for his fishing boat. Mr. Shiney spent hours at the lake pulling in huge catfish and teaching his boys how to bait a hook or use one of the new lures he'd bought that morning up at Lizard Lips. Mr. Jackson also came along by marriage. Mr. Jackson set up some sort of music pad out back in the old abandoned mobile home. He wired it up with huge amps, and a mic, and padded the walls with carpeting. Mr. Jackson would wail on his guitar all weekend at the Shiney J. Carlene, over at Lizard Lips, set up a gig for him to play on Friday nights in the summer. His boys play the keyboard and drums. Both Mr. Shiney and Mr. Jackson were obsessed with The Blue Things, an obscure Hays, Kansas, garage band that played psychedelic music during the 1960's. They spent hours practicing The Blue Things hits, including "Pretty Things – Oh" and

"Silver and Gold." Bobby Day had been the drummer for The Blue Things and as things will sometimes happen, it turned out that after the band broke up, Bobby found his passion for banging out beautiful handmade kitchen cabinets rather than banging on a drum. He opened up a cabinet shop in Lawrence, Kansas. Well, being as Kansas is sort of just one big small town, Bobby got wind of the doings down at the Shiney J in Toronto. He showed up one day and spent the evening playing with the Jackson and Shiney boys. Mr. Jackson confided to his brother-in-law, Mr. Shiney, that this was the best night of his entire life.

Tarot Cards

Esther was the most beautiful girl in Woodson County. She was the senior class high school prom queen. Every year, she was the Queen for the Toronto Independence Days parade, riding on the back seat of the 1964 Bonneville convertible owned by Homer's son, Tom. You know. Homer? Homer's grocery? Well, it closed after The Great Recession of 2008, but his son, Tom, lived outside of Toronto. Remember? He's the one with the cow shed where the pirate spiders hung out. Esther worked as a Licensed Practical Nurse in the nursing home over in Eureka, but she had an active business as a fortune teller on the side, reading palms and Tarot cards. Men from miles away, as far away as Cottonwood Falls, came around hoping to be the one Esther chose to marry. She had bankers and dentists and over-the-road truck drivers and men working on the new wind farms, trying their best to win her over. It wasn't until Jack came to town to do some tuckpointing on a brick building downtown that Esther took notice. He was from down around Grove, Oklahoma. He was rough. His hands were like sandpaper from all those years laying bricks and working with mortar. He had jet black hair and shiny black eyes, like deep moonlit pools. Esther fell hard and they ended up married. Took their honeymoon at The Rafael Hotel overlooking The Plaza in Kansas City. When asked why out of all these fine eligible bachelors, she would choose Jack, she smiled and said, "It was in the cards."

Sam and Lillian

Sam and Lillian had lived right across the street from each other since they were three years old. Sam's mother was single and she'd adopted Sam after resigning herself to being single, somewhat of a recluse, and now already 45 years old. After bouncing around since she was born, Lillian's mother decided that she'd do best by raising her little girl in a small town. Sam and Lillian became fast friends. Sam's mother was very strict and kept him on a short leash. She feared he'd take off with Lillian when they got to be teenagers. Lillian loved to explore down by the Verdigris River. Sam's mother feared he might drown in the river like her friend, Susan. Susan had gone and drowned in that river where it was hardly even three feet deep. Lillian's mother didn't mind much what Lillian did as long as she was home before dark. Lillian made adventures. She dreamed of adventures. She made tree forts and fairy houses. She made sculptures out of clay from the banks of the river. She made the old lady who lived next door practically jump out of her skin and have a heart attack when Lillian would jump out of nowhere and shout, Boo! When Lillian took off to go to the Art

Institute in Kansas City, Sam stayed in Toronto and took care of his mother. When Lillian went on a photo shoot to Costa Rica, Sam stayed home and swept the sidewalk. Lillian found her peace bouncing around doing this and that, some sort of adrenalin rush. Sam found his peace sweeping with a broom. When his mother died of a stroke at the age of 65, Sam took his inheritance and opened a specialty broom shop in Kansas City where he and Lillian lived together peacefully. He cleans and she dreams.

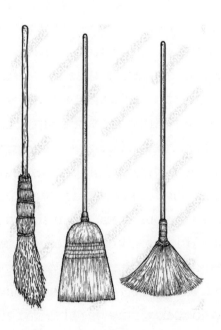

Long Live Larry!

Unbeknownst to even members of the Kansas Explorers Club, Toronto was not only off the beaten path but was also home to a settlement of Little People. Elves and Fairies have lived there longer even than the mound builder civilizations. The Elves found the area to be perfect with plenty of water and the Black Jack oak forests provided craggy, rocky ledges, with small cave-like spaces to live happily year-round. Humans had always lived there too, so it was easy to steal little things like a baby's sock to use as a sleeping bag or small stubs of candles to light up a long night. The Fairies loved all the mossy paths along the Verdigris River. These were Water Fairies and they rode the dragonflies that flitted over the sparkling streams. The Fairies had a banquet every year to honor one of the humans. It felt sort of like an alien abduction to Larry when he found himself coaxed down a trail near the lake. He couldn't say what drew him there, but there he was. He found himself sitting on a log surrounded by Fairies who tucked flowers in his hair and gave him honey nectar to drink. "Long live Larry!" the Fairies exclaimed. Larry was crowned King of the Fairies that year. When he asked why he deserved such an honor, the Fairies only giggled and explained that he had planted clover in his yard that year AND voted for Laura Kelly! Such an extraordinary Kansan! Hail, Larry, King of the Fairies!

Pi Day

In 1920, the population of Toronto reached an all-time high of 829 people. In 2020, the mayor announced a special celebration to commemorate this notable time a century ago. It was the Greatest Pie Contest and Auction ever to be held on Pi Day, March 14th, featuring 829 pies! The ladies at the Methodist church and the ladies at the Cowboy church joined forces to prepare. (No one mentioned the story about the one guy who had died after eating pie at a Methodist Church fundraiser). The great German pie artist, Karin Pfeiff-Boschek, traveled to Toronto to judge the event. She hosted pie art workshops where locals could learn to create rosettes, hearts, leaves, berries, stars, diamonds, and braids to decorate their pies. The mayor of Rockland, Maine, known as Pie Town USA, ran the auction. 829 pies were set out on tables running up and down the full length of Main Street. People came from as far away as Liberal, Kansas, and Mountain Home, Arkansas, to bid on pies. For one day, the number of people in Toronto swelled to 830. The highest price paid for a pie in the auction was $829. The Grand Prize went to a pie with 4 and 20 blackbirds.

"Sing a song of sixpence,
A pocket full of rye.
Four and twenty blackbirds
Baked in a pie.
When the pie was opened
The birds began to sing;
Was'nt that a dainty dish
To set before the king."

Feel Real Good
Real Quick

In the beginning, when Peggy and Clayton moved to Toronto, they didn't realize that they would be the only ones doing what they do. They picked Toronto as a place to land by opening up a *Rand McNally Road Atlas*, randomly, closing their eyes, and pointing a finger to the page, which, as it turned out, ended up being Toronto, Kansas. They had both grown up in St. Louis. Neither had ever been to Kansas, but after years of city life, the couple was ready for something new. Toronto sounded like it would be someplace sort of proper or at least a place of plenty. They'd looked it up on Google and found that the word "Toronto" means "plentiful" in Wyandot. They contacted the local and only realtor in Toronto, Tom Hibbard, and bought, sight unseen, a 5-bedroom house on 5 acres for $65,000. Their dreams coming true. Or so it seemed. Quickly settling in after moving the essentials from St. Louis and adjusting to the lack of internet, a grocer, or a gym anywhere around for miles, they hung up a sign in the yard and made-up flyers.

Feel Real Good Real Quick!
Mindfulness Counseling
Meditation
Eat right
Sleep Well
Find true love
Overcome all phobias

Well, being as there had been no psychologist anywhere around for miles, longer than no grocery, no gym, no school, word got out FAST and before Peggy and Clayton could even set up a new bank account, customers lined up, eager to get fixed from all manner of nervous tics, bouts of rage, skin rashes, fears of spiders and lingering resentments toward former school teachers. The Kansas Behavioral Sciences Regulatory Board got wind of the operation. Someone in Wichita who was used to getting Toronto folks driving three hours round trip for therapy reported them to the authorities. The Kansas Behavioral Sciences Regulatory Board shut them down real quick. Feel Real Good Real Quick changed their business model real quick and had customers help plant and grow peonies to sell for the busy Memorial Day activities at all the local and numerous cemeteries. Everyone swore that growing peonies really did make them feel real good real quick.

How to Grow Peonies Real Good Real Quick!

1. Don't plant too deep
2. Plant in a sunny location
3. Plant in soil that drains well. Peonies do not like damp feet.

Sandy

Summertime in Toronto is too damn hot and humid. One time, a pipe burst at Dianna's shack and no one discovered it for several weeks until water started seeping down the driveway into the street. It was hot and the whole house grew mold and mildew like old ladies grow whiskers on their chins. Unlike whiskers, mold and mildew can rot a house down to its bones. We spent a week cleaning everything with bleach. The mold hid between books on the shelves and in the back of the kitchen cabinet behind the boxes of detox tea and rice noodles. No matter how hard we tried, we were no match for Mother Nature. The same summer, high winds in a thunderstorm split a hackberry next to the house and a limb broke right through the roof into the old back porch that was used as a place for the grandkids to sleep. There was only one bedroom. Sometimes everyone slept outside in tents. Sandy's old man, Bill, patched the hole in the roof. Sandy lived down the street. Sandy had been in a terrible fire at the prison and her hands were both mostly scar tissue. Her fingers curled up permanent like claws. Sandy used the word "fuck" as a noun, verb, and adjective.

"That fuck better leave me alone."

"I fucked her up."

Or, "that fucking cat had another litter."

She already had 17 cats, 3 dogs, and Bill. She let Bill sleep inside her trailer house if it got real cold. Otherwise, he slept in his truck.

Golden Domes

After seemingly successfully creating a Center for Transcendental Meditation in a small farming community, Fairfield, Iowa, those die-hard meditators who wished to spread the Maharishi's truth had been searching for a place to build another set of Golden Domes and another Vedic City. Someplace that might be open to a culture like this. Bea Potts grew up in the unincorporated spot called Neal, just down the road from Lizard Lips. She left home at sixteen, hitchhiked, and after a series of boring events of no interest really, especially for a book of tall tales, she ended up in Fairfield, Iowa, working as a cook in the dining hall at Maharishi International University, serving tofu and dahl to the mostly Chinese teenagers who now made up the bulk of the student population, lured there by the promise of a transcendental education in the heartland of America. Well, Bea mentioned to the Dean of Development that Toronto, Kansas, might be just perfect for a new Center. Dean Bean (honestly, his real name) contacted the then-mayor of Toronto. Somehow, the cell phone connection was bad. All the mayor heard was some guy wanting to set up a Center for Condensation rather than a Center for Transcendental Meditation. The mayor hung up on Dean Bean, blocking any further calls from that number.

Rhinestones

When Frank, who had run the funeral parlor over in Yates Center, died, his daughter came down from Lincoln, Nebraska, to clean out his place. He lived upstairs at the mortuary. His daughter, Liz, never thought a thing about the corpses downstairs waiting for their final resting place, either over in the Rocky Ford Cemetery or the Cedar Bluff Cemetery. Folks seemed to have a preference for whether they wanted to lay eternally near water or up higher overlooking the woods. After selling the business to someone from Santa Rosa, California, who wanted to get away from the fires and raging heat, Liz started cleaning out her father's chest of drawers. Stuck way back in a corner, underneath his socks, she found an old photo, folded over in half as if to hide the image from anyone who might go digging around in his drawers. A photo of a woman, buck naked floating in a small pond. I mean, on her back, totally nude wearing only a rhinestone necklace. Liz looked carefully and realized immediately that this was NOT her mother. Later, a group gathered at the grave site for a small memorial. It was mostly other morticians, gravediggers, preachers, florists, and an elderly woman who seemed out of place. Liz studied her carefully and realized it was the naked lady from the photo! She made her way around the tent to the other side of the casket. The casket, of course, was top-of-the-line. By the time she got through all the condolences and hugs, the lady was gone. All she left was a rhinestone necklace hung over his marker.

Caw! Caw!

Eileen could speak Crow. She was not a member of the Crow tribe. She grew up in Toronto and she spoke with the Crows. She never knew when Crow would show up. She could be shaking a rug outside or hanging clean hankies on the clothesline and there would be Crow, sitting on the fence by the backyard gate. Eileen would ask, "Caw, Caw?" which meant loosely, "What's up?" Crow would tell her about the storm brewing to the south and about the truck which jack-knifed on the turnpike near Emporia. One day, Crow stopped by and brought Eileen a diamond ring. Crow told her to take an adventure. Eileen replied, "Caw, Caw!", which meant loosely, "You are such a good friend". She took the ring to a shop in Wichita and sold it for $7,000. Then, she booked a flight to Venice, rented a car, and drove down the Dalmatian Coast. Much to her surprise, when she spoke to a Crow in Croatia, Crow looked quite puzzled and asked her if she was American. Eileen queried, "Caw, Caw?", which meant loosely, "How did you know"? Crow replied, "You have a funny accent!"

An Invention

Credit for the use of the Phillips screwdriver is given to Henry Frank Phillips from Portland, Oregon, who was the force behind getting the automobile industry (specifically Henry Ford) to adopt both the crosshead screw and driver which carries his name.

What is not so well known is that John P. Thompson, born and raised in Toronto, actually invented the cruciform screw and the screwdriver for it during The Great Depression of the 1930s. Like so many others, Thompson headed west during The Depression where he met Phillips, a businessman who was making money hand over foot selling medicines like Phillips Milk of Magnesia. Thompson and Phillips met at a diner and got to talking. Thompson told Phillips about his invention and Phillips offered to buy the patent for $1,000. Well, that was too much money for Thompson to turn down, so he sold it quickly. Phillips made off like a bandit making millions off the Phillips head screwdriver and Thompson, basically, got screwed.

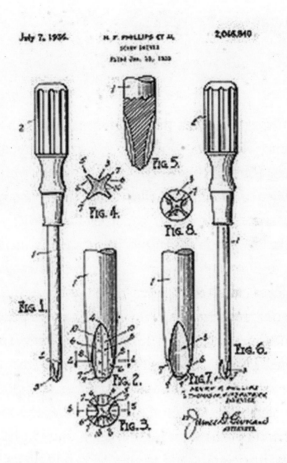

Sasquatch

Back in 2021, residents of Toronto were in a state of panic when for eight days in a row, dogs and cats all over town and even out in the county were found dead with their guts torn out and left for the vultures. Local law enforcement, the county sheriff, and the Kansas Department of Wildlife and Parks were called in to solve the mystery. One night, Mickey Moose (his actual, real given birth name) was driving home from the lake after enjoying a few intimate moments of kissy face with his girlfriend. Mickey slammed on the brakes when a very large giant hairy monster about eight feet tall ran across the road right by the entrance to the Cross Timbers State Park. Big Foot! Sasquatch! (You may remember earlier in this book that Dianna was saved from a terrible Kansas Winter Wind Blizzard by Sasquatch.) Once again authorities dismissed the story, but word got out. Big Foot hunters or Sasquatchers (as they are known) from everywhere descended on Toronto setting up camp out at the lake. Anti-vaxxers showed up wanting to learn more about how Sasquatch survives without the use of modern medicine. Film producers, talk show

126

hosts, celebrities, members of the Flat Earth Society, ancient astronaut theorists, and all manner of thrill seekers came in droves. Totos rented out rooms in their homes and the churches filled their basements with Sasquatchers. The old school was opened up and used as a headquarters for meetings, press releases, data analysis, and sales of Sasquatch novelty items. The place became a Covid super spreader epicenter, but this deterred no one. Within a month, abandoned houses were purchased, a new housing development sprang up on the western edge of town and a Walmart Supercenter opened across the highway from Lizard Lips. The population grew from 281 to 102,810 by the winter. And that is the end of this story.

128

End Notes

I had to do it. I Googled the question.

"Do Lizards Have Lips?" Lizards don't have lips, neither do turtles, salamanders, frogs, snakes, birds (relatively obvious) or even mammals like rodents. Lizards can smile though."

From https://neeness.com/do-lizards-have-lips/

A different opinion comes from the University of Toronto vertebrate paleontologist Robert Reisz, who explains that lips help to protect teeth, in part by helping to enclose them in a moist environment where they won't dry out. Crocodiles, which spend their time submerged in water, don't need lips for protection. "Their teeth are kept hydrated by an aquatic environment," Reisz says. However, reptiles with lips, such as monitor lizards, typically live on the land where their teeth require different protection. How cool is it that Reisz is at the University of Toronto! Canada, of course.

My search led me to discover a wealth of trivia about lizard lips:

> A lip balm called Lizard Lips

> A book titled *Beware of Kissing Lizard Lips* by

Phyllis Shalant

> An action figure called Lizard Lips Lenny
> A film titled *Smoked Lizard Lips* from 1991
> A popular song titled "Lizard Lips" by the band Good Food
> An instrumental jazz piece titled "Lizard Lips" by Tardo Hammer
> A three-piece covers band from the UK called The Lizard Lips
> A Succulent called Aloe Lizard Lips
> A chicken fingers dish called Lizard Lips on the menu at the Winking Lizard Tavern which actually has 14 locations in Ohio
> A beer called Lizard Lips on tap at the West Flanders Brewing Company in Boulder, Colorado
> A gummy candy treat called Lizard Lips
> A dock leveler known as a Lizard Lip is a hydraulic loading dock with an extendable lip used to reach the back of trailers. The Lizard Lip dock leveler creates a barrier that stops lift trucks from driving over the edge of the dock.

About the Author

I grew up in a family of storytellers. Well, some people would call us liars. The bigger the exaggeration, the better!

I wrote this a few years back and I think it explains best why I would come up with such a book as this.

My Tribe:
We gather round the table and tell bits and pieces of this story and that story, or something about cousin Mary Beth or Uncle John. We all have dogs and cats,and brick patios and gardens rambling with gooseberry bushes and money plants and castor beans and geodes and quartz crystals. Generally, we collect things: books, *National Geographics*, angels, bird feeders, recipes, baseball caps, guns, costume jewelry, guinea hens, poetry, travelogues, and friends. Oh, they say that long ago we had lots of land and lots of money, but being the way we are in this family, we couldn't hold on to it, dancing around, drinking and gambling, and so forth. We are teachers, tinkerers, librarians, scientists, artists, writers, musicians, peddlers, engineers, dabblers, farmers, doctors,

bricklayers, electricians, midwives, and mechanics. We like … dumpster diving, scuba diving, rock hunting, treasure hunting, singing in the choir, singing in the shower, fishing in the lake, fishing for a compliment, a pot of soup and some, well, some don't have a pot to piss in!

You can find me at home just off the banks of the Kaw River in North Lawrence, Kansas. I've written two other books that are quite different. *Write to the Source ~ A Journaling Guide for Recovery* and *Spice It Up ~ An Herbal Extravaganza.*

One last note – For any of the graphics I have used in this book, "no copyright infringement is intended."

If you have any tall tales, or lizard stories to share, feel free to contact me: irisgarden9@gmail.com

132

The Ice Cube Press began publishing in 1991 to focus on how to live with the natural world and to better understand how people can best live together in the communities they share and inhabit. Using the literary arts to explore life and experiences in the heartland of the United States we have been recognized by a number of well-known writers including: Bill Bradley, Gary Snyder, Gene Logsdon, Wes Jackson, Patricia Hampl, Greg Brown, Jim Harrison, Annie Dillard, Ken Burns, Roz Chast, Jane Hamilton, Daniel Menaker, Kathleen Norris, Janisse Ray, Craig Lesley, Alison Deming, Harriet Lerner, Richard Lynn Stegner, Richard Rhodes, Michael Pollan, David Abram, David Orr, and Barry Lopez. We've published a number of well-known authors including: Mary Swander, Jim Heynen, Mary Pipher, Bill Holm, Connie Mutel, John T. Price, Carol Bly, Marvin Bell, Debra Marquart, Ted Kooser, Stephanie Mills, Bill McKibben, Craig Lesley, Elizabeth McCracken, Derrick Jensen, Dean Bakopoulos, Rick Bass, Linda Hogan, Pam Houston, Paul Gruchow, and Bill Moyers. Check out Ice Cube Press books on our web site, join our email list, Facebook group, or follow us on Twitter. Visit booksellers, museum shops, or any place you can find good books and support our truly honest to goodness independent publishing projects in order to discover why we continue striving to "hear the other side."

Ice Cube Press, LLC (Est. 1991)
North Liberty, Iowa, Midwest, USA
Resting above the Silurian and Jordan aquifers
steve@icecubepress.com
Check us out on Twitter and Facebook.
www.icecubepress.com

Celebrating Thirty-Two Years of Independent Publishing.

To Fenna Marie, BMSW—
for all the reasons,
for all of time, you
are always the ultimate GK!